Contents

Any words appearing in the text in bold, **like this**, are explained in the Glossary.

Communications

Communications are different ways of talking to people. Television, radio, newspapers, post, telephone and the **Internet** are all types of communication.

Communicating by post

Millions of people send letters or parcels to each other by post every day. The letters give information of one kind or another.

This woman works for the postal service in the United States. She is delivering letters and small parcels.

www.heinemann.co.uk/library

Visit our website to find out more information about **Heinemann Library** books.

To order:

 Phone ++44 (0)1865 888066

 Send a fax to ++44 (0)1865 314091

 Visit the Heinemann Bookshop at www.heinemann.co.uk/library to browse our catalogue and order online.

First published in Great Britain by Heinemann Library, Halley Court, Jordan Hill, Oxford OX2 8EJ, a division of Reed Educational and Professional Publishing Ltd. Heinemann is a registered trademark of Reed Educational & Professional Publishing Ltd.

OXFORD MELBOURNE AUCKLAND JOHANNESBURG BLANTYRE GABORONE IBADAN PORTSMOUTH NH (USA) CHICAGO

Designed by Visual Image
Illustrations by Visual Image
Originated by Ambassador Litho Ltd.
Printed in Hong Kong/China

06 05 04 03 02
10 9 8 7 6 5 4 3 2 1
ISBN 0431 11284 3 (hardback)

06 05 04 03 02
10 9 8 7 6 5 4 3 2 1
ISBN 0431 11291 6 (paperback)

British Library Cataloguing in Publication Data

Royston, Angela
   Post. – (In Touch)
   1. Postal service – Juvenile literature
   I. Title
   383

Acknowledgements

The Publishers would like to thank the following for permission to reproduce photographs:
Aviation Images: p21; Canon Printers: p25; Corbis: p28, Colin Garratt p20, Tim Hawkins p12, Matthew McKee p7, Minnesota Historical Society p4, Paul Seheult p5, Patrick Ward p6; Parcel Force: p5; Philip McCollum: pp13, 22; R.D. Battersby: p26; Royal Mail: pp14, 15, 17, 19; Sheena Verdun-Taylor: p27; The Stock Market: p23; Stone: Bob Schatz p24, Lawrence Migdale p4; Tudor Photography: p8; US Postal Service: p18.

Cover photograph reproduced with permission of Corbis.

Every effort has been made to contact copyright holders of any material reproduced in this book. Any omissions will be rectified in subsequent printings if notice is given to the Publisher.

This postal worker is helping to get each of these parcels on to the next stage of its journey through the post.

Postal services

Many different people collect and deliver letters and parcels. **Postal services** are the companies that organize the post.

This book shows you how the postal services work. It shows the many stages that a letter has to go through from posting to delivery.

Writing a letter

The post is both cheap and simple for people to use. You do not need special machines – just a pen and paper! Millions of letters are posted every day.

Posting a letter

To post a letter to a friend all you have to do is write the **address**, stick on a **stamp** and drop the envelope into a postbox.

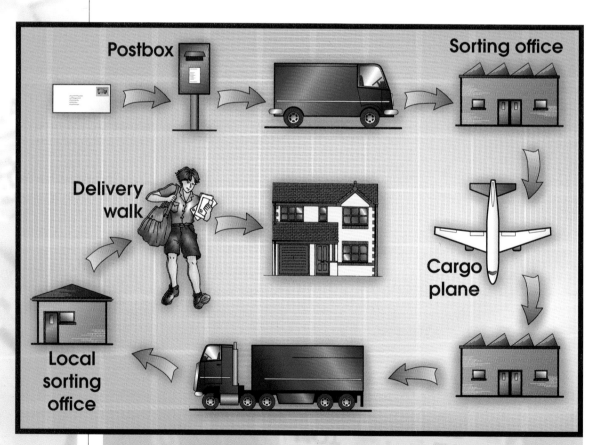

Postbox

Sorting office

Delivery walk

Cargo plane

Local sorting office

This is how a letter gets from a postbox to the person you are sending it to. The **sorting office** uses the address to send it to the right place.

This woman is sorting letters into pigeon-holes. Each pigeon-hole is labelled with the name of a particular city or area.

Addresses

The **postal service** must know the address of the person the letter is going to. The address tells them exactly where someone lives – the name or number of the house or block of flats, the street, and the town or city.

Receiving a letter

A day or two later, the letter is pushed through your friend's letter-box or dropped into a box at the end of their drive.

Postal services

A **postal service** is a huge organization. When you post a letter, it has to go through many stages before it is delivered to your friend. Many people help it on its way.

Post on the move

Vans, lorries and trains carry the post from one **sorting office** to another. Planes carry post from one country or state to another. Vans deliver parcels and some urgent letters. Most letters are delivered by people on foot.

Different kinds of letter carry different **stamps** and stickers. Some letters and parcels travel long distances.

The motorcyclist has brought this bag of letters to an airport in Australia. The special mail plane is ready to carry them on their way.

Different kinds of letter

If your letter is urgent, you can send it using an express service. This delivers the letter faster than other letters, but it costs more. Valuable items are given special treatment too. If they are lost, the postal service pays for the value of the item.

Circulars

A circular is a letter which is copied and sent to many people. Circulars can be sent at a cheaper rate, but they take longer to be delivered.

Stamps and franks

You have to pay the **postal service** to collect and deliver your post. One way to pay is to buy **stamps** and to stick them on the front of the letter or parcel.

The post office

Heavier letters and parcels cost more to post. The heavier they are, the more they cost. A worker at the post office weighs the parcel and works out how much you have to pay. You must make sure that you have wrapped the parcel well and **addressed** it properly.

Heinemann Library
Human Resources
100 N. LaSalle St.,
Chicago, IL 60602

You can write the address on a letter or parcel. Or you can type it on to a label and stick the label on. It does not matter as long as the address is clear and accurate.

Postmarks

The post office **franks** every letter and parcel it receives. The franking machine prints a **postmark**. It gives the date, time and place the letter was received at the post office or the **sorting office**. Some large companies have their own franking machines.

The postal service in each country prints and sells its own stamps. Stamps often have pictures of things that are special to the country.

Collecting the post

A postbox has a narrow slit. It is big enough to let a letter or small parcel through, but it is too small for someone to reach in and take any letters out.

Emptying the postbox

Postal workers empty postboxes at least once a day. They unlock a door in the box and collect all the letters inside. Postboxes at some post offices have a **conveyor belt** that carries letters away.

A girl posts her letter in a postbox. Each postbox has a list of the times the post is collected from it. The last collection from here is at 5.30 pm.

Postcodes

Every **address** includes a **postcode**. The postcode helps the **postal service** to sort your letter more quickly. It also makes sure that the letter goes to the right place.

In Britain, the postcode shows the area and group of houses in the street. In the United States and Australia, the postcode shows a particular area within a state.

You cannot post a large parcel in a postbox. You have to take it to the post office.

Sorting offices

A **sorting office** sorts the post according to where each letter or parcel is going. Thousands of items arrive at the sorting office each day. In smaller sorting offices, the post is sorted by hand. In large offices, machines do much of the work.

Machines

Vans bring the heavy sacks of post to the sorting office. **Conveyor belts**, slides and rollers move letters and parcels from place to place.

Post of all shapes and sizes arrives at the sorting office. Here it is being moved by a conveyor belt.

This drum helps to sort the post. As it spins around, it throws the post to the edge. The drum has slots in it, but only letters are thin enough to fall through the slots.

Sorting by size

The first stage in sorting the post is to separate it by size. Ordinary letters, large letters, small parcels and larger parcels are put into different groups. A huge drum separates ordinary letters from the rest of the post.

Ready to sort

Ordinary or **standard letters** can be sorted by machines. Other letters and parcels have to be sorted by hand.

The facing machine

Standard letters are put into a facing machine. The machine turns them the right way round with the **stamp** at the top. It can do this because most stamps have **fluorescent** ink in them. It only shows up under a special light.

Another machine then prints the **postmark**.

This machine is printing a postmark on the letters.

Codes

Some computers can read **postcodes**. The computer turns the postcode into a **machine code**. The machine code is often a **barcode**, like those that shops use. Or it is a pattern of dots.

The machine code is printed in fluorescent ink. You can often see it on the envelope.

This computer cannot read the postcode. So an operator reads it and types it into the computer.

Sorting machines

Letters marked with a **machine code** pass to the sorting machine itself. The sorting machine reads the machine code and finds the place name which matches the code.

The sorting machine then pushes the letter into the right container. The machine is so fast it can sort ten letters every second.

Each of these containers collects the letters for a particular place. When a container is full, it is taken away. An empty one is put in its place.

This postal worker is pushing a container of post into a van. All of these letters and parcels are going to the same city or area.

Sorting by hand

Large, fat letters and parcels are difficult to sort by machine. They are usually sorted by hand instead. Postal workers read the **addresses** and throw the parcels into the right containers.

Sorting parcels by machine

Some **postal services** do have machines that can sort parcels. As the parcels move along a **conveyor belt**, the machine guides them on to belts that carry them straight into post vans.

Transporting post

All day and all night, trucks and vans take the post to and from **sorting offices** all over the country.

Mail trains

In some countries, special mail trains speed the post from one part of the country to another. Postal workers re-sort the post from different sorting offices. When the train stops at a station, they unload all the sacks for that area.

This man is re-sorting letters on a mail train. He puts all the post for each city or area into its own sack.

Air mail

Post travels from one country to another on special cargo planes. Large countries, such as Australia, the United States and Canada, use cargo planes to fly post quickly from one state to another.

Cargo planes

Cargo planes do not have many seats. Instead they use the space inside the plane to carry goods. Post is taken from sorting offices to a post centre at an airport. Then it is loaded on to the planes.

This plane is carrying letters and parcels, which will be delivered across the United States.

Delivering post

Post is taken to the main **sorting office** in a city or area. There it is re-sorted and sent to local sorting offices. Here it is sorted street by street into postal 'walks'.

Postal walks

It takes many postal workers to deliver the post. Each one delivers the post along a particular walk or route. A walk always starts in the same place and goes to each **address** in the same order.

This postal worker is using a van to deliver post. Workers normally do the same route every day.

Van, bike or foot

Some walks have too much post to carry by hand. Companies and offices may have sackfuls of post every day. The post for these walks is loaded into post vans and delivered by the driver.

Postboxes

Most homes have a letter-box in the door or a box at the end of the drive. Some people collect their own post from a numbered postbox at the post office.

Large parcels like this one are delivered to your door by van. This girl is signing a form to say that she has received the parcel.

Post by Internet

Today, telephones and computers carry messages much faster than by letter. So you might think that there is less post to deliver. But the opposite is true.

Direct mail

Some companies that sell things do not have shops. Instead they post out catalogues of their goods, or show them on the **Internet**. You can order what you want by telephone or on a computer. The goods are delivered by post.

This woman is using her computer to shop. She decides what to buy and orders on the computer.

Postal service websites

Postal services have **websites** on the Internet where you can see what services they offer. You can also look up and check information, such as **postcodes**.

Remote printing

Remote printing is a special service used by some companies. The company supplies a leaflet and list of **addresses**. The **sorting office** prints, addresses and delivers the leaflet.

This printing machine is in a sorting office. The machine prints leaflets for a company. The postal service then addresses the leaflets and delivers them.

Not just post

Post offices and postal workers often do more than handle the post. Some post offices are also local shops that sell groceries as well as **stamps**.

Licences and pensions

In post offices in Britain you can pay for **licences** for cars and televisions. You can apply for a passport here too. The post offices also pay **pensions** and other **benefits**.

The post office is often at the centre of village life. People come here for almost everything they need.

Looking out for people

Postal workers often get to know the people who they deliver post to. They know who is elderly or disabled. They notice if someone does not answer the door when they should be there. If they think something may be wrong, they call the police.

People use the post office for different things. Some people have a bank account at the post office. Others pay bills through the post office.

Postal times

Here are some important events in the history of the post.

2000 BC In Ancient Egypt people are paid to carry messages.

1st century AD The Romans set up a **postal service** that covers their **empire**.

1200s Merchants set up their own postal services in several parts of Europe.

1627 The first postal service that everyone can use is set up in France.

In the USA, the Pony Express began in 1860. Riders like this one rode fast horses to carry the post from one **relay station** to another.

1700s In Britain, special mail coaches carry post to and from London.

1840 The first **stamps** are used in Britain. The stamp costs the same however far the letter has to go.

1850 Railways and steam ships carry post faster than ever.

1918 Planes are used for the first time to deliver mail in the USA.

1960s Machines are used to sort and handle letters.

Here, the pilot of one of the first mail planes helps to load his plane with post.

Glossary

address list which shows the building, street, town and area where you live

barcode printed stripes which a computer can read

benefit money paid by the government to people who have special needs

communication way of sending and receiving information

conveyor belt moving band which carries things from one place to another

empire group of countries ruled by another country

fluorescent giving off light

frank stamp with a machine

Internet worldwide network of computers

licence piece of paper that says you are allowed to do something

machine code symbols that a computer can read that show the postcode

merchant someone who buys and sells things

pension money paid regularly to an elderly person who no longer works

postal service organization that collects, sorts and delivers letters and parcels

postcode numbers and letters that show where you live

postmark frank that shows where and when a letter or parcel was posted

relay station a stopping place on the way to somewhere

sorting office place where letters and parcels are grouped according to where they are going

stamp piece of paper which shows how much postage has been paid

standard letter letter which is less than a certain weight and about a certain size

website collection of information about a particular subject stored on the Internet

Index